Benjamin F. DeCosta

The Pilgrim of Old France

or the Huguenots on the Hudson, 1613-14. To which is added The stormy

petrel and other pieces of verse

Benjamin F. DeCosta

The Pilgrim of Old France
or the Huguenots on the Hudson, 1613-14. To which is added The stormy petrel and
other pieces of verse

ISBN/EAN: 9783337287641

Printed in Europe, USA, Canada, Australia, Japan

Cover: Foto ©ninafisch / pixelio.de

More available books at **www.hansebooks.com**

The Pilgrim of Old France

OR

The Huguenots on the Hudson, 1613-14

TO WHICH IS ADDED

The Stormy Petrel and other Peices of Verse

New York

1894

PRIVATELY PRINTED

In Memory

OF MY MOTHER AND MY HUGUENOT ANCESTORS.

DECEMBER, 1894.   B. F. DE COSTA.

The Pilgrim of Old France on the Hudson, 1613=14.

"While in their company we conversed with the first male born of Europeans in New Netherland, named Jean Vigné. His parents were from Valenciennes, and he was now about sixty-five years of age."—[Journal of the Laba-dists, Sept. 24, 1679.]

ERE yet the rod of Holland ruled
   Around Manhattan's shore,
The Gallic Pilgrim, scarred and worn,
   His household thither bore.

A Pilgrim cast in homely mold,
   Plain son of grand Old France,
Yet fearless as the bravest knight
   That ever broke a lance.

What burgh his errant ship sent forth,
   Or what her master's name,
No legend now remains to tell
   Or sound her ancient fame.

Yet long the brave ship ploughed the wave,
  By many a peril fraught,
'Till ev'ry league of sea was passed
  And nigh appeared the port.

The port where Verrazano furled ²
  The Dolphin's storm-torn sail,
When searching far for fair Cathay,
  He met the wintry gale.

Then Louis' silver lilies waved
  Proud o'er this harbor wide,
Well nigh a hundred ³ years before
  The "Half Moon" stemmed the tide ;

While floating free from Gomez' peak, ⁴
  The castles of proud Spain
Told where her storm-tossed caravels
  Found refuge from the main.

The Narrows passed, DeVigné's ship
  Glides smoothly up the bay,
The Red Man safely piloting
  The strangers on their way.

And now they breast the North-land stream,
  The swirling Hudson's tide;
The mighty stream that mountain brooks
  Give ocean for his bride.

Shatemuc by Mohicans named,
  In savage times afar;
Ere yet a ship of Manitou
  Had crossed the harbor bar.

By Spain "Rio Montana" known,
  But "San Antoino"
By men of Lusitania,
  Four hundred years ago.

Here, all unknown, DeVigné came—
  Storm-swept, with straining mast,
Far forth from old Valenciennes,
  By adverse fortune cast.

The incense-breathing wilderness
  Delights the Huguenot;
And anchored safe mid vernal scenes
  The past is soon forgot.

E'en though a past that only Hate's
   Inhuman skill could frame,
The headsman's axe and guillotine,
   Or martyrdom's fierce flame.

Full kindly fortune held her charms
   Before his tear-dimmed eye,
And hope revived with new-born strength,
   Beneath the New World sky.

For while fair France the Pilgrim spurns,
   He finds a welcome here,
And round the ship the bark canoes
   Like sea-gulls linger near.

Then landward points the painted chief,
   To where his camp-fire's smoke,
Of savage hospitality
   And simple manners spoke.

Anon, with signs and gestures rude,
   But unaffected joy.
He proffers with a Red Man's zeal,
   Rich peltries for a toy.

Thus kindly bade, the Huguenot,
  Adown the ship's side bore
His faithful wife, fair Adrienne,
  And sought the shining shore.

His landing place no column marks;
  Perhaps some sandy beach,
Where glad waves gently rolling break,
  And sea-shells slowly bleach.

Here soon the skilful Huguenot,
  A roof tree and a hearth,
Built, strong in conscious innocence,
  Nor feared the Red Man's wrath.

Nor watch nor ward the Pilgrim knew,
  No castle's frowning wall;
No armed men the Indian awed,
  With brazen bugle call ;

But kept the rule the loving Christ
  Had taught the Pilgrim well,
And thus among rude savages
  In amity to dwell.

His cottage stood with open door,
  Where sang the sparkling rill,
The Master finding sure defence
  In Huguenot good will.

Then through the forest's fragrant air,
  The voice of childhood rang,
And e'en at eve a lofty Psalm,
  DeVigné household sang.

And thus the Pilgrim of old France,
  Condemned by kings to roam,
Found on Shatemuc's breezy bank,
  A new and peaceful home.

For ere the Leyden Pilgrims ` trod
  Dear Plymouth's sacred Rock,
The Huguenot had hither led,
  His small but reverent flock :

Close following in Hudson's track,
  To find Shatemuc's name,
Of Indian story changed to sound
  The Englishman's fair fame ;

Since first of modern mariners,
  The sailor of Bow Bells,
Through Juet's English, " crude and quaint,
  The river's beauty tells.

The Summer's labors quickly passed
  And Autumn's forests told
The New World's rare magnificence,
  In crimson flecked with gold.

Secure, he scans the maple boughs
  With martyr fire ablaze;
These pale, and lo! they sweet lead in
  The Indian Summer's haze.

So when the Frost King comes, well pleased
  He sees bright crystals trace
In figures on his window pane
  Valenciennes' fair lace.

Soon Spring the ice-bound world sets free,
  And Summer in her pride
Returns once more to glad his heart
  And strew her favors wide.

Thus changing seasons came and sped,
 Yet changeless peace they brought,
And every day the Pilgrim's prayer
 With honest labor wrought.

Now, hampered by no feudal code,
 No law of Church and State,
He lived the life that Nature lives
 Secure from Old World hate.

Reposing safe along upon the shore
 Where broad Shatemuc rolled
The Pioneer of grand old France
 Gained wealth worth more than gold.

For here the Pilgrim, banished far,
 Found, while he tilled the sod,
The freedom grand old France denied,
 And safely worshipped God.

The Stormy Petrel.

THE birds of the air have their nests,
   But, Petrel, whence dost thou roam?
From clefts in St. Kilda's rude rocks,
   Or cliffs flecked with Orkney foam?

What eyrie, O bird, dost thou claim,
   And how dost thou rear thy young,
What prospect first dawns on their sight,
   By what breeze is their lullaby sung?

Strange rover of tireless wing,
   In sunshine and tempest the same;
Dame Carey's own Chick [1] thou art called,
   But whence came this singular name?

The Redbreast is sacred to Thor, [2]
   The martial god of the North,
And the woodsman who makes him his mark
   Must fear the Immortal's dread wroth.

But who was the Mother of Eld,
  O, Petrel, who heard thy lone cry:
The wierd one who made thee her own,
  And pledged her protection for aye?

How wove she the mystical spell
  That masters the sailor's mind,
The hot, headlong passion restrains,
  And renders the rough nature kind?

Thou guardest the mystery well,
  Locked up in thy silent breast,
But full many a curious thing
  Is known in thy downy nest.

What ancient traditions are thine!
  Thou sighted the purple sail
The captain of Zidon unfurled,
  To catch the Atlantic gale.

The "Long Ship" of venturesome Leif,
  Thou gaily gave easy chase;
A thousand hazy years ago
  Thou dared that Vinland race.

With Colon thou wandered far,
  When seeking Cathay in the West,
While his sailors in breaking their bread,
  First offered to thee of their best.

A sacred oblation they deemed
  The tribute that stilled each fear,
Fresh courage affording when hymns
  Were poured on the Virgin's ear.

The track of the Cabots thou knew,
  And great Prima Vista saw, [5]
But explorers thou never once told
  The bounds of that wonderful shore.

The sea-roving, keen-eyed hawk
  Flew lazily many a mile,
To pilot Betancourt's tall ship
  Safe into the Azor Isle. [6]

But Avant Courier, canny bird,
  Thou ne'er skim the foaming wave,
And to-day, as when Tyrians steered,
  Thou follow, not lead the brave.

The dragon-beaked ship of the North,
　　With the galley of Galilee,
Now tower proud castles afar,
　　Charmed palaces on the sea.

But no changeling thou, strange bird,
　　Evolution e'er shuns thy kind;
For still, as on primitive floods,
　　Thou, changeless, emprise the wind. [7]

The Nun in the Belfrey.

"O CARRY me up to the hill-top"
   Said the dying Ursuline;
"Up to the Sunny Convent
   Where the air is opaline."

" Yes, carry me up to the Belfrey,
   For Mount Benedict's Fair-view;
O carry me, strength is failing,
   My Sisters dear and true."

"They say that the widespread prospect
   Is so beautiful and grand;
O carry me up this morning,
   To see our Promised Land."

Then they carried her up to the Convent,
   Up the dizzy Belfrey stair,
And placed the feeble recluse
   In a Nun's antique arm chair.

And then, as up on Pisgah,
  Moses gazed o'er Palestine,
The Nun from out the Belfrey
  Viewed far and wide the scene.

Below the Mount a village
  Lay smiling scattered round;
And, closer, past the Convent
  The slow canal-boat wound.

The shaggy heights of Medford,
  And Prospect's storied Hill
With Harvard's classic towers
  A noble distance fill,

The Ten Hills Farm in order
  It's fields and furrows show;
While Bellingham its summit
  Lifts crowned with spring-tide glow.

Anigh the heights of Bunker,
  So verdant and so free,
Told where the patriot yeoman
  Plied his deadly musketry.

Afar the Tri-Mount City
  Held up its noble dome
And, full proud, the Modern Athens
  Told the culture of its home,

Beyond, the noble harbor,
  Gemmed thick with shining isles,
Spread, land-locked, safe to seaward
  Nine broad and placid miles.

The waters of the Mystic
  Mirrored many a charming scene,
And the Charles, a silver serpent,
  Wound through marsh and meadow green.

Thus shone the lovely picture
  That filled the Nun's dim eye;
Nor dreamed the faithful Ursuline
  An hour of ruth drew nigh.

She little recked the torches
  That the Sin of every Age,
Intolerance—was binding
  For the Bigot's purblind rage.

She kenned not that the prospect,
. So peaceful and so fair,
Would glow and throb one midnight
  With the burning Convent's glare.

She knew not that the Belfrey,
  Which crowned Ursula's Hall,
'Mid smoke and sparkling cinders,
  Would blaze and writhe and fall.

But while she gazed, deep musing,
  Her brow seemed all impearled
With radiant, new found beauty,
  Shed from out another world.

'Twas the favored gift of Heaven,
  The resplendent aureole,
That shines around the forehead
  Of the Chosen Sainted Soul.

And thus the Nun unmindful
  Of the day of bale to dawn,
Came down the Belfrey stair case,
  And rested on the lawn.

Again she viewed the landscape
  So tranquil and so bright,
And deemed it but the guerdon
  Of the Land of Endless Light;

While the Convent of Ursula
  A type and pledge should be,
Of each true Nun's sweet cloister
  In the true Nun's "ain Countrie."

NOTES.

The Pilgrim of Old France on the Hudson, 1613=14.

1. The Dutch West India Company did not send out its company of Colonists, composed chiefly of French Protestants, until 1623. De Vigné came in 1613.

2. Verrazano, commissioned by Francis I., visited the Hudson in 1524.

3. Henry Hudson, the Englishman, of Bow Bells, London, came to the River in 1609. The River was discovered nearly a century before, by the Spaniards or Portuguese.

4. Estevan Gomez the Portuguese, visited the River in 1525, and named it in honor of the St. Anthony. It appears "Rio San Antonio," in the map of Ribera, 1529. Also on early maps as "Rio Montana," and "River of the Mountains."

5. Valenciennes was early a Huguenot centre, where Protestants endured many trials, some of which, as elsewhere in France, by political complications, they brought upon themselves.

6. Old Navigators often speak of the fragrance of the air on approaching the American coast.

7. The story of De Vigné was told by the writer in a Paper read before the New York Historical Society in

1893. The first household, north of Virginia, was established by De Vigné.

8. The Plymouth Pilgrims came over in 1620, but De-Vigné in 1613-1614.

9. Hudson's voyage was described by his Mate, Robert Juet, o' Limehouse, London.

The Stormy Petrel.

1. The author has never been able to learn the origin of the name of this strange bird.

2. In Northern mythology the Redbreast is sacred to the god of war, who appears with a red beard. The story is, that whoever kills a robin will be struck by lightning.

3. Lief Erickson, who discovered America.

4. The sailors of Columbus paid great respect to the Stormy Petrel.

5. John and Sebastian Cobot discovered America before Columbus saw the mainland.'

6. The Hawks piloted this navigator to the land.

7. The Petrel always follows a ship, sometimes for hundreds of miles.

The Nun in the Belfrey.

This Convent stood on Mount Benedict in East Somer-
ville, near Boston, and was destroyed by cruel incendi-
aries on the night of August 13th, 1834. Before it was
finished the Nun s lived in a house at the foot of the hill.
When nearly completed, a Sister passing away with con-
sumption, asked to be carried up to the Belfrey, to view
the exquisite prospect, and see what the Nun s regarded
as their Promised Land. See "The Story of Mount Benedict," by the Author.

On Seeing a Cardinal Flower.

Lines suggested during a quiet day in the country. The
reference is to the military honors the writer saw paid to
a Cardinal on entering the Vatican.

Up sprang the Papal Legion
   At the watchful sentry's call,
While clang of arms resounded
   Through the grand palatial hall.

"The Cardinal ! Make ready !"
   And soon in order set
The brilliant platoons bristle
   With the burnished bayonet.

In trailing robes of office
   The great prince-prelate comes,
The musketeers saluting,
   At the roll of Roman drums.

With lordly eye and bearing
   Monsignore bows his thanks,
And lifts his hat of scarlet
   As he passes through the ranks.

Anon the prelate faded ;
  E'en while upon the stair
He vanished with the Legion
  And the Vatican in air.

So fades all human splendor
  In days of calm retreat,
When faith looks out serenely
  From religion's sacred seat.

And thus where shone the courtier
  In dazzling, bold relief,
I saw that Holy Jesus,
  Erst bowed by pain and grief;

But now the Man of Sorrows,
  Supreme in Edom's pride,
A crowned King was coming,
  His robes in Bozrah dyed.

All-glorious His apparel
  In that triumphant hour,
And thus for Christ the Conqueror
  I name this crimson flower.

The Cliff at Highland Light, Cape Cod.

O'er the shifting sand,
Of the sparkling strand
The jutting cliff uprears its head ;
Bastioned with gray
Alluvial clay,
And stained with dingy red.

A storm-sculptured steep,
Whence the swallows peep
From their ports beneath its crest ;
And where far away,
From the cold, salt spray
They build their sheltering nest.

'Tis the seabird's haunt,
Where the deep-sea chant
Swells up forevermore;
And the surf's hoarse chime
Keeps measured time
As it breaks along the shore.

In a sheltered reach
Of the oozy beach
Lies a shattered, grass-grown beam ;
'Tis some brave ship's mast,
That the Typhoon's blast
Laid low in the warm Gulf Stream.

Here the driftwood pile,
From many an isle
Twixt Roque and Malabar's verge,
Heaped high on the shore
Shall voyage no more
Nor toss in the tumbling surge.

When the sunlight fades
Night's gathering shades,
Seek the cliff's gray, caverned side ;
And far inward creep,
Where they sink to sleep,
Till Aurora rolls in on the tide.

Then the gloomy hosts,
Like belated ghosts,

Upstart and fly swiftly away ;
     And the old cliff gleams
     With the golden beams
Of Phœbus, good of the Day.

St. Michael and all Angels.

Angelic warders safe defend
    The chosen ones of God,
And where their farthest footsteps tend
    These warders first have trod.

The Child's good angel e'er beholds
    The Father's face above :
The same good angel softly folds
    O'er Age his wings of love.

Great Michael's swift, embattled band,
    A holy, God-sent guard,
At home, abroad, on sea and land
    Maintain their watch and ward.

Along the Hudson's shining banks,
  And on the mystic Nile,
As e'en in Palestine their ranks
  Shine forth in martial file.

With thoughts of love they sway the mind,
  But charge with unseen spears
The unseen spirits, demon kind,
  That throng from gloomy spheres.

Lord, let Thy angels guard from ill
  When e'er we wake or sleep,
And while we aim to do Thy will
  Their faithful stations keep.

Battle Hymn of the White Cross.

Arm of the Lord, in strength
  Stretch forth from out the sky,
And cause by Thy dread might
  Each foul-born foe to fly.

Behold Abaddon's Host,
  In serried ranks arrayed,
And swift against his front
  Flash forth Thy battle blade.

The Arch Fiend's brazen brow
  With awful terrors blanch,
While mailéd angels fast
  Their darts of lightning launch.

Alone, in vain we fight;
  In vain, O Mighty Arm,
We draw a mortal sword,
  And sound the war's alarm.

Reveal Thyself on earth,
  And banish, conquered, thence
The haughty hordes of vice,
  By thy Omnipotence.

Arm of the Lod, in strength
  Charge back defeat and loss,
And bright with triumph crown
  The Sinless Christ's White Cross.

The Lighthouse.

On the dizzy height,
In its robe of white,
A tower of strength the Lighthouse stands
With its granite base,
And strong staircase,
And Lantern girt with iron bands.

The pillar of old
O'er the ancient Fold—
A flame by night and cloud by day—
Through forty years
Of shadowy fears
Led doubting Israel on her way.

Thus Highland Light,
By day and night,
Lifts o'er the sea its cheerful sign ;
A snow white shroud,
A firery cloud,
A mystic messenger benign.

Nick and the Priest.

To the popular apprehension, "Nick," with "Old" pre-
fixed, is synonymous with Satan. Yet Nick is one of the
appellations of Odin. The individual himself, by northern
antiquaries, is considered one of the descendants of the
Asgard heroes, being deemed a person in whom many
good as well as some evil qualities are combined. He was
thought at times to assume a variety of forms, chiefly for
the purpose of mischief, and in the Old Norse legend, on
which the following *brochure* is founded, he is represented
as a beautiful youth, with golden curls, possessing all the
capacities of a water-sprite.

An aged priest of austere mien,
  Whose locks by time were silvered o'er,
Went forth to walk, and in his hand
  A sturdy staff he bore.

When passing near the river's brink
  This man of God by chance espied
A sprite, hight Nick, in royal garb,
  Disporting on the tide.

A harp was in his jewelled hand,
  And loose his magic mantle hung,
While skilfully he touched the strings,
  And sweetly harping sung:

"The Lord, the only God, is great,
 And freely every mercy gives;
O hope, my soul, for well I know
 That my Redeemer lives."

Amazed the hoary priest replied,
 "O Nick, dost *thou* dare hope in God?
Ere such as thee find grace, this staff
 Shall bud like Aaron's Rod."

Nick heard, and sorrow filled his soul;
 No more he sung the glorious lay,
But bowed his head upon his breast,
 And flung his harp away.

The priest passed on, but lo, his staff!
 The dry stick feels a heavenly power—
It buds, the verdant leaves burst forth,
 Then brightly blooms the flower.

And while he walks new twigs appear,
 Obedient to the Lord's device,
Until he seemed some saint who bore
 A branch from Paradise.

This marvel smote the old man's heart;
　He rightly read the mystic sign,
And backward went, with trembling steps,
　To own the truth Divine.

And coming to the river side,
　He humbly thus addressed the sprite:
"Now well I know that all may find
　Acceptance in His sight;

This blooming branch is God's decree,
　Within my heart no doubt now lurks;
O magnify the Lord who reigns
　In mercy o'er His works !"

Nick heard the words, and saw the branch,
　Joy filled his tear-stained eyes ;
He seized his silent harp and sang
　A song that reached the skies.

Though aged then the priest went forth,
　And every land wherein he trod,
He preached his late-found faith with words
　That burned with fire of God.

On Finding a Rare Flower Near the Pyramid.

Poised on my camel, I securely rode
Mid scenes where, anciently, the Pharaohs trode.

The mighty pyramids on either hand
Looked down, majestic, o'er the sea of sand.

The Sphinx, dread mystery, upreared its head,
Above the wreckage of dim ages dead.

Sahara's desert, far as eye could see,
Spread drear and barren without shrub or tree,

No sign of verdure in this vast expanse
The keen eye greeted ranging wide askance.

The gentian heavens, true Egyptian sky,
Arched o'er a wilderness now parched and dry.

The death that wantoned in the neighb'ring tomb,
Had struck with barrenness fair Nature's womb.

And yet as, patiently, afar and wide,
My camel journeyed, I a marvel spied.

"What ho, Mohammed!" while my Bedouin stands,
"See yonder jewel in the Afric sands!"

A mass of mineral this marvel seemed,
As out the *débris* its rare beauty gleamed.

"Look now, Mohammed, some gem lost erstwhile
By Ramses marching 'neath great Ghizeh's Pile."

The agile Bedouin thus full quickly sped,
And raised the jewel from its lowly bed.

A gem reflecting amethystine ray,
A desert flower that had bloomed to day.

Such flowers sweet budded in Sahara's flame,
Ere Thotmes conquered or the Hyksos came.

These gems in beauty nobly rank before
All gems that Egypt's haughty monarchs wore.

Thus the great Author of Creation bids,
O'ershadowed grandly by vast pyramids,

This lustrous flower in its wealth to grow
Where sand streams wander with their mystic flow ;

While fierce Siroccos burn the red wild o'er,
And range the desert as in days of yore.

Learn, then, the Lesson of the desert flower,
Born where old Cheop's grand memorials tower :

No life so baren, and no waste so bare,
That may not blossom with those virtues rare,

That find their fellow in the miracle
The dusky Bedouin ever knows so well ;

Fair traits that beauty and effulgence bring,
Beyond the splendor of a Memphian King.

In Gethsemane.

Close by the Garden's sunny glade,
Beneath the ancient Olive's shade,
In sad but sweet Gethsemane,
I muse its awful mystery.
A mystery we ne'er forget,
A mystery Evangels set

In frames of tears, but tears impearled
By splendors from the unseen world ;
Tears that the Sinless God-Man wept
As faint and lone the Watch He kept,
His followers failing in the hour
When foes advance and storm-clouds lower.

What sorrows smote our Saviour's heart,
While kneeling, desolate, apart
We may not know, but yet believe
'Twas through His sorrows we receive
That wondrous gift of joy and peace
Which brings a sinful soul release.
And yet the mystery abides,
With sphinx-like silence it derides
Sad questioners who tread the path
Christ trod when breasting human wrath ;
For each disciple, like his Chief,
Must know the fellowship of grief.

Grant us, O God, at last to know
In full life's meaning here below;
Yet in Gethsemane to hear,
Sweet falling on Faith's eager ear,

Some measure of Angelic song,
Sung clear by Heaven's enraptured throng,
In passing sweet glad minstrelsy,
Illumining the Mystery ;
Proclaiming how each transient pain
May work for our eternal gain,
And thus in Christ's sad Garden rise
A fair and joyous Paradise.

Sonnets.

TO ALEXANDER CRUMMELL, D. D.,
ON HIS JUBILEE, 1894.

The Field of Zoan in proud Pharoah's land
Saw wonders scattered by Jehovah's hand,
The shackles breaking when His awful tread
Filled ancient Egypt with immortal dread.
Thus in the New World, as along the Nile,
God woke to freedom thousands slaved erstwhile,
A nation quaking when His sovereign might
Afro-America gave Manhood's right ;
And through our borders on this day we see

A Crummell honored in his Jubilee,
The kindly Nestor of a rising Race
Still spared and faithful in his sacred place,
While sober learning and religion twine
The well-won laurel round a brow benign.

OUR DORCAS.

'Twas Dorcas dead, on Joppa's rugged shore,
Whose many charities they counted o'er ;
But Dorcas living is the theme I sing,
And cheerful tribute to her worth I bring ;
For twice, though Moslem, Koran-charmed she march
Athough the desert by Siroccos parched,
The good-wife bearing, genuine Frankish frieght,
All free from stubbornness and prankish hate ;
Which toilsome tourists know, if not quite blind,
Is not the custom of the camel kind.
Thus mid the Pyramids Dorcas won a name,
Her kindly temper ever found the same ;
And so, good Dorcas, I would speak thee well
In bidding Eygpt and the Nile farewell.

THE KINGDOM.

Kingdom of God ! who would not be
In that grand principality
A subject whose far-shining days,
Exhaustless, lapse in songs of praise ?
There love is law, and rules alone,
Eternal as the crystal throne,
Whose beams of clear, supernal light
With endless day shut out the night ;
While joy pervades each tranquil breast,
Brief toil exchanged for endless rest ;
Where peaceful banners float unfurled,
In mem'ry of a conquered world :
Kingdom of God ! who would not be
Crowned in that Principality.

THE MISSING TONE.

Addressed to the bells of Christ Church, Boston, on
hearing the Chimes on a quiet evening when loitering on
Breed's Hill.

Bells of my boyhood, which at eve and prime
From out yon tower flung the mellow chime,

Afar swift flying with i's rythmic call
To glad observance of high festival ;
Once more thy sweet tones, as in youth's bright day,
Through trembling air paths o'er the swift Charles stray
And, tuned to numbers of immortal cheer,
Pour their full choral on my waiting ear.
But though no clearness hast thou lost, fair bells,
A tone, deep treasured in my memory tells
That thou no longer in thy silvern peal
To youth and gladness as of erst are leal,
And while the hillside I now weary tread,
I vainly listen for that tone : 'tis dead.

BY THE MANGER AT BETHLEHEM.

The proud astronomer with boasted ken,
May scorn the witness of those noble men
Who hither journeyed from the East afar
Led by the splendor of a new-found star .
Yet kneeling, rev'rent, in the rock-hewn cave
Of Holy Mary, where the world to save,
The Sinless God-Child in deep need was born,
And destitution of dishonor shorn,

We seek the wisdom that alone makes wise,
And guides the pilgrim who would read life's skies,
Which blaze at mid day with an occult sign,
To modern Wise Men teaching truth benign ;
That by the Manger where the Magi trod
The soul, truth-hungry, may be led to God.

FAREWELL TO JERUSALEM.

City of David, Home of Kings farewell !
Towers of Zion, where Christ's praises swell
In solemn measure floating far and fair,
On sunbright Palestine's calm, listening air ;
Farewell again with thy sweet memories,
Thy soft bells chiming in the Spring-tide breeze,
Thy walls receding from my wishful sight
And domes evanishing in throbbing light,
Farewell, thou City of my fondest hope,
That all too late upon my vision broke,
And all too early with slow step I leave
With sense of loss I vainly seek to heave
From off my breast ; yet hoping, is it vain,
To come with joy some distant day again.

JERUSALEM AGAIN.

O Hill of David, Seat of our great God,
Where spell-bound, musing, I so lately trod,
Shall I, in time, again be hither brought,
Again take up the thread of broken thought?
Again stand, reverent, 'neath those azure skies
To which the God-Man raised His Holy eyes?
Again look forth from Olivet's grand Mount,
And muse once more by Silo's broken fount?
Failing in this, my portion be to see
The New Jerusalem above, the Free,
Of which the City on fair Zion's Crown
With all its sanctity and high renown,
Is but the archetype, the Symbol bright
Of Zion glowing in eternal light.

SALISBURY CATHEDRAL.

For purity and perfection of style, called the Parthenon of
English Cathedrals.

With air majestic Salisbury's spire upsprings
O'er Plain and City, while the grand arch sings

Its *Sursum Corda* for the passer by
Who views the minster from afar or nigh.
The mystic masons, brought across the sea—
Bold Derham's fancy built in symmetry,
And glad devotion toiled to rear the pile,
The loyal brother, free from greed and guile,
Full level laying where the Master trod,
Each stone by Calvary's measuring rod ;
Till, course on course, the fane above the foss
Assumed the outlines of that Holy Cross,
Whose god-like virtue smote what dark Stonehenge
With Druid Altar would in vain avenge

BISHOP-STEAD THE SEAT OF DELAWARE.

Where speeds the Brandywine a hill-born tide,
Its chiming surges waking far and wide
The rock-rent valley, with the dulcet tones
Of dear old Shakspere's sweet "enamell'd stones,"
An ideal mansion rules amid tall trees,
Whose tuneful branches teach the wand'ring breeze
To answer deftly with true Antiphon
Swift-rolling Brandywine's bright Carillon.

What is thy scutcheon, gravely-ordered pile.
With glowing Chantry where, apart awhile,
Earth's Pilgrim, resting 'mid its beauties fair,
Full reverent offers each due Praise und Prayer?
Thy name on Brandywine is Bishop-stead :
There, equal, Learning and Religion tread.

THE IRISH-AMERICAN SHAMROCK.

The tiny shamrock from fair Erin's Isle
That languished drearily alone erstwhile
Near ancient Derry's rock-indented coast
Where haughty James so vainly spent his boast,
Now thrives luxuriant in its new-found home,
Born safely westward o'er the ocean's foam,
Each day attended by a loving hand,
Hand of a pilgrim from Old Ireland
Which seems invested with some mystic spell
That Erin's Shamrock swift obeys full well.
Pray tell the secret of this wondrous change,
All sweet attended by a beauty strange.
I know the secret, 'tis no occult art :
The exiled Shamrock warms to Irish heart.

HOMEWARD BOUND.

The home-bound Pilgrim from the Holy Land,
With joy approaches his, dear native strand
And looks far westward 'cross the purpling sea
At sunset, asking if there yet may be
In view some outline of the New World's shore,
Amid the fulgence spreading grandly o'er
The clouds of crimson with pure silver lined,
By bright gold bordered, gleaming God-refined.
Thus when life's sun-set softly draws anigh,
May I stand watching an immortal sky,
And reconnoitre the horizon's verge
Above the ocean's calm, transfigured surge,
For signs emblazoned mid the clouds impearled
To mark the borders of the Better World.